From Bound 2 Found

From Bound 2 Found

RENNEÉ J. JOHNSON-HUBB

XULON PRESS

Xulon Press
2301 Lucien Way #415
Maitland, FL 32751
407.339.4217
www.xulonpress.com

Printed in the United States of America.

ISBN-13: 978-1-54562-854-6

"Bring my soul out of prison
That I may praise your name;
The righteous shall surround me
For you shall deal bountifully with me."
– David (Psalm 142:7)

Prayer for when the place that is supposed to be a place of refuge becomes a prison.

Dedications

I would like to dedicate this book to my children: Kaviona and Keyon, and my sister Sharitta. Thank you for enduring the hardships with me, for being there every step of the way, and for loving me during my unlovable days.

To my sister Robin, people would be surprised to know that there was a time when we were like total strangers with no love for one another. Literally, two weeks before my mom passed, Mom was standing in the kitchen and told us, "If you don't get along when I'm gone, I will come back and haunt you." Through God's love and His healing power, we have grown from unlovable to lovable.

This may sound strange, but I would like to thank my past. Though it was filled with pain, a lack of forgiveness, a lack of understanding, wrong choices, and times I could not stand to accept myself, it molded me into the woman I am today.

> *My brethren, count it all joy when you fall into various trials, knowing that the testing of your faith produces patience. But let patience have its perfect work, that you may be perfect and complete, lacking nothing.* (James 1:2-4)

Author's Thoughts

My message is to all of you who are lost, hurting, and bound in a life where you are constantly unsure what crisis the day may bring. I, too, was bound in that life, but I want to help you understand that you were created in the image of God and He has a plan and purpose for your life. Understanding this will allow you to become comfortable in your own skin and cast away the bondage in your soul caused by the damaging words spoken over you. Then you will be able to love another and be loved the way God intended. This is very important to being able to move from "Bound 2 Found" so you can fulfill God's great plan and purpose for your life.

To the young mothers who are experiencing unbearable conditions in their lives, I want you to know I understand feeling as though you cannot make it, as you are bombarded with the stressors of the world and unsure of where your next meal will come from. I promise you, if you hold on to God's unchanging hand and endure the hard times, trouble does not last. Better days are coming. Jesus is with you and has promised to never forsake you.

For the young ladies who are dating, I want to warn you that once you open the door to pre-marital sex, you open yourself to a battle you will fight for a life time. Learn from my mistakes and save yourself for your husband. As a daughter of God, know that the beautiful life He has planned for you in a marriage relationship designed by Him is worth the wait.

> *For I know the thoughts that I think toward you, says the* L*ORD*, *thoughts of peace and not of evil, to give you a future and a hope.* (Jeremiah 29:11)

INTRODUCTION

Bound to My Past

"Trials teach us what we are; they dig up the soil, and let us see what we are made of." – Charles Spurgeon

"From Bound 2 Found" was given to me by God. This book was birthed out of the trials, adversity, life's obstacles, and choosing my own path. Through the Lord's guidance, writing this book helped me let go of my past, which had kept me in bondage. As I began to write this book, God used it to heal the wounds in my heart and mind.

As I reminisced over my life, God showed me how my past had kept me bound and left me unable to move forward with His plan for my life. As I wrote stories about losing everything and being homeless, drinking, clubbing, having an abortion, and two children by the age of eighteen, I saw the bondage caused by my self-destructive lifestyle. Then losing my mother, trying to commit suicide, being involved in multiple destructive relationships, lying, stealing, and generally suffering from low self-esteem, my bondage escalated until I felt there was absolutely no hope for me for any kind of productive life.

Being bound by all of these things, it was impossible to love myself or anyone else for that matter. The enemy was determined to rob me of my future by binding me to my past.

However, that is not the person I am today. Through the grace and mercy of my Lord and Savior, Jesus Christ, I am no longer bound by my past.

I am a new creature in Christ!
I have moved from Bound 2 Found!
I have learned that in God,
all things work together for my good!

January 22, 2003: I distinctly heard a voice say, "Go tell her you love her!"

I didn't know who said that but I was tired, so I proceeded to the elevator and answered, "I'll tell her tomorrow."

This was my first encounter hearing the small still voice of God.

I was also about to discover that tomorrow is not promised.

2002 was the year I truly believe God ordained for my mother and I to restore our relationship. The woman who provided for me, cared for me, and showed amazing strength was now vulnerable, sick, and needed my help. I took FMLA in 2002 to accompany my mother to her doctor's appointments. My mom always had long thick flowing hair and we noticed that her hair started to fall out. We cut her hair short. Taking my mom to her Dialysis appointments several times a week, to a Rheumatoid Arthritis specialist, and several other doctors' appointments kept me busy week after week.

It allowed me to see how sick Mom really was, but she never complained. She worked two weeks prior to her death (to help cover her medical bills). My last moment with my mom was one I will never forget. We were laughing and joking. Then the doctor came over and said, "Ms. Hubb, your vein collapsed again. We have to perform a procedure for you to receive dialysis."

Mom said, "No, I'm tired." I tried talking with her and explaining that she needed to get it done. She said, "Renneé, they have poked me and worked on me enough."

January 23, 2003: Approximately five o'clock in the morning, I received a call that would change my life forever. It was my grandmother.

She yelled frantically in my ear, "Get up here to the hospital!"

My grandmother told my sisters and me that we had to make the decision by the end of night about taking my mom off life support. She had gone 24 hours without any brain activity. We made the decision and I left the room. My sister Robin came out of the room and told us my mom was gone. It was like a ton of bricks hit my chest and I went black. I woke up surrounded by friends and my dad. I desired to talk, but I was unable to talk about it for a week. During that time, I saw my mom in my dreams wearing all white telling me to come with her. Not being able to communicate to people what was going on was hard. During that time, I thought about committing suicide many times to be with her. I realize now that it was the enemy trying to make me abort what God designed for my life.

I really believed that God would perform a miracle and heal her. He did heal her, but on the other side. I am thankful that God allowed me the opportunity to repair our relationship, but I also realize how much time I missed by holding onto things and allowing the enemy to use the unforgiveness to hinder me.

> *"Many people ruin their health and their lives by taking the poison of bitterness, resentment and unforgiveness,"* says Joyce Meyer. *"I always looked at forgiving people who hurt me as being really hard. I thought it seemed so unfair for them to receive forgiveness when I had gotten hurt. I got pain, and they got freedom without having to pay for the pain they caused. Now I realize that I'm helping myself when I choose to forgive."*[1]

---

[1] https://www.joycemeyer.org/everydayanswers/ea-teachings/the-poison-of-unforgiveness

I had not yet learned the truth expressed in Ephesians 4:26-27 that tells us not to let the sun go down on our anger or give the devil any such foothold or opportunity. I discovered it is hard to hate one person but love another. It is hard to treat anybody right when our heart is not right. Even people I wanted to love were suffering from my bitterness, resentment, and unforgiveness.

CHAPTER 1

Bound by Childhood Shadows

There are events or people in our lives that cast a shadow over us whether they have done it intentionally or unintentionally. When their shadow overshadows ours, it can cause us to lose sight of who we are. It often leads to an identity crisis in our lives that we carry with us into adulthood. To overshadow means to tower above and cast a shadow over, conceal, or obscure.[2]

"Overshadowing" through verbal abuse is the negative effect of verbal descriptions spoken over a child by an authority figure such as a parent or a teacher.[3] Verbal abuse when we are children can affect the way we see ourselves and impact our lives well into adulthood. Not only are we likely to experience an identity crisis, we may also develop low self-esteem. In some cases, children of verbal abuse can also show self-destructive behavior such as cutting and other self-injurious acts. A recent study demonstrated that verbally abused children develop interpersonal problems, physical aggression, and delinquency at a higher rate when compared to others. Due to this

---

[2] Powered byOxfordDictionaries© Oxford University Press

[3] https://en.wikipedia.org/wiki/Verbal_overshadowing

aggression, they may hit other children or may quarrel with their classmates.[4]

HURTING PEOPLE HURT OTHERS.

A new study by Florida State University researchers has found that people who were verbally abused as children grow up to be self-critical adults, prone to depression and anxiety. People who were verbally abused had 1.6 times as many symptoms of depression and anxiety as those who had not been verbally abused and were twice as likely to have suffered a mood or anxiety disorder over their lifetime according to psychology Professor Natalie Sachs-Ericsson, the study's lead author.[5]

My Shadow Story

My mother and I had a love / hate relationship. When we argued, it could escalate to physical contact at times. For years, I held unforgiveness in my heart due to the amount of emotional abuse I had suffered growing up.

Numerous occasions during my childhood and as a young adult, I wanted to kill myself. My depression and suicidal thoughts started as a child—always believing that I wasn't pretty, I was too fat, and no one loved me. One time, I worked up the courage to tell my dad what I was feeling and he comforted me, but it was only a temporary relief from the inner conflict I experienced on a daily basis.

---

[4] http://www.theparentszone.com/child-development/emotions/what-are-the-effects-of-verbal-abuse-on-children/

[5] https://www.fsu.edu/news/2006/05/22/invisible.scars/

My mom always provided materially for us, though I was basically raised by my sister, Robin. We knew she loved us, but the communication factor did not exist.

When my mother was in a relationship that caused us to move abruptly from one state to another state so my mom could be closer to that man, I began to witness how controlling someone could really be of another human being. I saw how it can even make you take children from a previous relationship and try to make them fit with a new relationship. Unfortunately, I also saw how a man could verbally and physically abuse a woman that he claimed to love. That relationship caused the bitterness, dislike, and loss of respect for me towards my mom.

One situation stands out the most and affected me more than the others. My mother and her boyfriend were arguing and he hit my mother. Outraged, I stood up to him and he hit me, too. We went back and forth verbally and physically until he finally left. At that moment, I made up my mind that I would defend myself against any kind of verbal and physical attack no matter who the aggressor was or how intimidating they might be.

This incident also caused anger to build up in me towards my mother because she would not defend herself against this abusive man. She just kept moving us from place to place and remained in the relationship with him. I did not understand why we had to move, why we had to leave our family, why I had to leave my dad, and why we were staying with someone who did not seem to really want us there.

Our moving to follow the man my mother was in relationship with took us into Virginia and over three hours away from my Dad. This made it difficult for him to visit, so he did not know the things that happened in our house.

No one knew that I battled wanting to kill myself. Leaving everything I knew and constantly hearing "you're fat, you're not smart," and other derogatory comments, and living in a house that was beyond dysfunctional left me with such low esteem that I searched for ways to numb the pain.

On top of those inner feelings of low self-worth, cursing and yelling were my mom's ways of communicating. I do not think people understand what they are speaking into their children when they say things like, "you're not going to amount to anything." Looking back, I believe my mom spoke what was being spoken to her by the abusive man who continued to claim he loved her in spite of constantly degrading her emotionally, verbally, and physically. As I grew older, my sibling and I began to take a stand and fight for her.

At one point, I became angry with my mom for putting up with the abuse I began to physically attack her. My mom and I got into one fight, which I truly regret. This one altercation with my mother ended when the police were called. They asked me to leave even though I was only fourteen years old at the time. I packed my stuff and went to stay with my God-sister and her mother. That week was peaceful. I felt like I could get used to this type of life and environment.

However, it was short lived. My mom called and said that I had twenty-four hours to get home or she was going to report me as a runaway. I returned home, though I really did not want to be there. That is when I turned to alcohol for relief from my pain. I started to slowly sip on my mother's alcohol. I found that by drinking the alcohol, I could escape to a world where I could fulfill my ambitions. I had a desire deep in my heart to be a singer, so I would drink the alcohol, turn on my music, and daydream about being on stage performing to escape the craziness around me.

My grandmother's house was mom's haven. If things got so bad with my mother's boyfriend that even she could not stand it, we would go to my grandmother's house. We knew not to speak about what happened, so my grandmother had no idea what was going on at home. She never asked any questions, she just opened the door and was happy to see us whenever we showed up on her doorstep.

Mom Arrested

My sister and I came home from school one day and my aunt was there. She said we were all going to stay with her for a couple of days. I was in the seventh grade at the time. My sister and I begin to ask questions, but my aunt refused to tell us what was really going on. We later discovered that our mother had been arrested for credit card fraud.

We were still residing in Virginia during this time, but we were told that we would be staying with my grandmother in Maryland for the next year. I had grown accustomed to living in Virginia, and though we were living in a dysfunctional environment, I considered it my home, my school, and had my friends. Now, I was being told were moving back to Maryland to live with my grandparents in their one-bedroom home. My sister and I slept in the living room on a pullout sofa.

Relocating back to Maryland was a rough transition for me. The style, the kids, the environment, and the school system were all different. My eighth-grade year was the worst year of my young life. I felt like an outcast trying to fit in with kids who had known each other from elementary school and I was bullied and threatened. I shared what was happening with my dad and he told me that running away was not an option. I was forced daily to face kids who talked about my weight and generally made me feel like an outcast. I never really felt like I was fitting in.

Looking back, I can see how important it is to train your child up at a young age about how beautiful they are and help them understand that they are made in the image of God. Society can make or break a child by defining who they are at an age when they are very susceptible to peer pressure.

My mom was sentenced to a year in Federal Prison and sent to Texas. For that entire year, we could not talk to or see our mom. To deal with not seeing her and the bullying I was experiencing at school, I began to have thoughts about killing myself. I did not know how to express myself other than through anger, bitterness, and saying very hateful things.

Overwhelmed with unforgiveness and hatred, my heart was hardening. I did not understand why mom left, why I could not see her, and why I had to leave my friends. The year she was incarcerated, I was rebellious, disobedient, disrespectful, and very rude to my grandparents. I owe them so much for caring for me in spite of my destructive behavior.

It seemed like every time I would get used to something being semi normal, things would drastically change. Anger was my way of protecting myself. When my mom was released from prison, she came home to a child totally different from the one she once knew.

I did not realize how unforgiveness had begun to overtake my heart and fill it with anger and bitterness. I was becoming so bound by unforgiveness that it was hard to love anyone including myself. Left unchecked, unforgiveness can breed so many other negative emotions. Fear, anxiety, depression, suicidal thoughts, and self-harm may surface, as well as drug and alcohol abuse. It often takes years of intense counseling to get to the root of these destructive behaviors.

The one highlight of that year when my mother was in prison, though, was I was living closer to my dad. He spoiled me rotten during that time. I admit I totally took advantage of it, too. I had a mindset of life is not fair and I deserve to be compensated for all my pain and suffering.

My dad really stepped in when my mom went to prison. He was a provider not only for me, but he would do for my sister and cousins as well. I did not want for anything materially during that time. He made sure I had the latest clothes and shoes, my hair and nails were done, and I had money to spend.

One day, I was riding with my dad and we drove past a private school. I told my dad I would love to go there. Three weeks later, my dad pulled out a packet with a welcome letter in it saying I was going to start attending that private school. I was blown away, but I did not understand the wonderful opportunity he had given me until I got older.

BECOMING AN OVERCOMER

As we conclude this chapter, take a few minutes to think back over your own life experiences. Review the circumstances I have shared and compare them with yours.

First of all, consider this definition of a shadow. It is defined as a dark area or shape produced by a body coming between rays of light and a surface that casts a shadow over or overshadows.[6] Verbal and physical abuse can cause this "shadow" in your life.

Verbal and physical abuse are often associated with physical and emotional symptoms such as:[7]

[6] Powered byOxfordDictionaries© Oxford University Press

[7] Adapted from healthyplace.com

Chronic pain including migraines

Stammering

Fear, anxiety, depression

Sleep and eating disorders

Irritability and anger issues

Alcohol and drug abuse

Suicidal thoughts and attempts

Self-harm

Assault behaviors

Look at the list above and reflect on the things that have tried to overshadow you, especially if they have resulted from your childhood verbal or physical abuse.

How did these "shadows" affect you physically and mentally?

____

____

____

How did these "shadows" impact the decisions you made in your adolescence and adulthood?

____

____

____

How did they keep you bound?

____

____

____

Read Luke 4:17-21.

What did Jesus say God the Father sent Him to do?

____

____

____

How does this relate to overcoming the "shadows" that have tried to overshadow you?

____

____

____

Understand the power that you have to overcome the things that try to overshadow you by studying God's Word.

Read Luke 10:19.

What did Jesus say He has given us so that we can become overcomers?

____

____

____

Read Jeremiah 29:11.

What is God's promise to you?

____

____

____

I also had unforgiveness overshadowing my life. I pray you learn from my mistakes and take these steps to deal with any unforgiveness in your life, so it will no longer keep you bound or give the enemy a foothold in your life.

1. **Decide** – You will never forgive if you wait until you feel like it. Choose to obey God and steadfastly resist the devil in his attempts to poison you with bitter thoughts. Make a quality decision to forgive, and God will heal your wounded emotions in due time (see Matthew 6:12-14)

2. **Depend** – You cannot forgive without the power of the Holy Spirit. It is too hard to do on your own. If you are truly willing, God will enable you, but you must humble yourself and cry out to Him for help. Ask God to breathe the Holy Spirit on you so you can forgive those who have hurt you.

3. **Obey** – *The Word tells us several things we are to do concerning forgiving our enemies:*
   - **a.** Pray for your enemies and those who abuse and misuse you. (see Luke 6:27-28).
   - **b.** "Bless and do not curse them" *(Romans 12:14).* In the Greek, to bless means "to speak well of" and to curse means "to speak evil of." You cannot get over it if you continue to talk about it. Proverbs 17:9 says that he who covers an offense seeks love.[8]

---

[8] https://www.joycemeyer.org/everydayanswers/ea-teachings/the-poison-of-unforgiveness

Begin keeping a journal of how God uses my story and His Word to begin to open your mind and heart to His love and healing power in your life. Focus on overcoming the things that try to overshadow you.

Isaiah 61:3 says Jesus came, "To console those who mourn in Zion, To give them beauty for ashes, The oil of joy for mourning, The garment of praise for the spirit of heaviness; That they may be called trees of righteousness, The planting of the LORD, that He may be glorified."

Understand the power that you have to overcome the things that try to overshadow you because **Luke 10:19** says, "Behold, I give you the authority to trample on serpents and scorpions, and over all the power of the enemy, and nothing shall by any means hurt you."

Now more than ever, kids are faced with peer pressure, media influences, and bad information from all angles. As Ralph Waldo Emerson said, "One of the biggest achievements we can have in life is to be who we really are."

"Peer pressure is pressure you put on yourself to fit in!"
– Jeff Moore[9]

[9] Jeff Moore is an entrepreneur, educator, and motivator driven to help people realize their own potential for personal greatness, healthy relationships, inspired living, and meaningful contribution. https://everydaypowerblog.com/2017/12/01/peer-pressure-quotes/

CHAPTER 2

Bound by Past Decisions

"I am convinced that every effort must be made in childhood to teach the young to use their own minds. For one thing is sure: If they don't make up their minds, someone will do it for them." – Eleanor Roosevelt, First Lady, USA[10]

I had my first sip of alcohol at the age of fifteen as I tried to deal with the pain in my life. Then, at the age of fifteen, I discovered it was a way to be like everyone else. I did not realize that decision would lead me down a road of destruction. My decision to take that first drink opened that door and it lead to years of alcohol abuse. I lived for the weekends. I would drink and party from 6 p.m. on Friday night until 7 a.m. Monday morning and repeat the cycle every weekend. I remember going out one night and waking up at 6:30 a. m. in front of my house in my car. My mom was banging on my driver side window, telling me to turn my car off and get in the house. I do not even remember driving home. I chose alcohol as my way to escape the pain and disappointment in my life and trying to fit in with others. My life became bound by this and other poor decisions.

[10] https://www.whatchristianswanttoknow.com/top-15-christian-quotes-about-decision-making/#ixzz57D0Gz8cL

At the age of fourteen, I lost my virginity. I was talked about and made fun of because I was a virgin. Not understanding that being a virgin was a blessing and not knowing that having premarital sex would cause me to have a life long battle of fighting my flesh, I gave into the peer pressure around me. The enemy convinced me that what God had designed to be special was keeping me from being accepted by my peers. I allowed the negativity from my peers to overpower what God had blessed me with and gave up my virginity.

I was headstrong and did not have someone to mentor me or provide a good example of what a functional family and marriage should be. I made a poor decision. I made a choice, but it was a poor choice. I decided at fourteen that I was grown and I should be allowed to make my own decisions. I told my mom I was going out and there was nothing she could do to stop me.

As my rebellion turned into more bad decisions, at the age of fifteen I became pregnant with my daughter, Kaviona. Though many advised me not to keep my baby, I was determined to raise my child no matter what. I did not understand I was not mature enough to raise a baby. In fact, it turned out I would literally be growing up with my daughter.

At that point, my life changed forever. My father stopped talking to me and my world crashed in around me. I went from being Daddy's little girl to being rejected by him. He would not answer or return my calls and did not even attend my high school graduation. Rejection from a parent can put you in a place mentally that can destroy you. Though I was devastated, it caused me to make a vow to myself that I would love my child unconditionally.

I thank God for Romans 8:28 which says, "For we know that all things work together to them that are the called according to his purpose, to them that love Him." Though I suffered from the rejection of my father, things completely turned around in my relationship with my mother. In fact, I learned unconditional love from my mother during this time in my life. When I became pregnant with my daughter, my mother made sure I ate well, she helped me with doctors' appointments, she helped me find childcare, and she never turned her back on me.

However, once again when given a choice, I made another poor decision. After I gave birth to Kaviona, I wanted to go right back into my old lifestyle. My mom did not want me to spend the night out clubbing and partying now that I had a baby to care for. I would argue with her saying I could make my own decisions and I would go out if I wanted to. My mom grew tired of arguing with me and she told me that if I wanted to spend the night out, I needed to find a place of my own. So, I packed up my daughter and we left.

Not understanding the consequences of moving in with a man I was not married to, who had no job and no life skills, I began to suffer mentally and physically. This dysfunctional relationship lasted for the next six years of my life. Our relationship became more and more destructive and my life began to look just like what I had grown up with and vowed my children would never have to experience. There was fighting, verbal abuse, and all the other dysfunctions that go with such a lifestyle.

A year after I moved out of my mother's house, I graduated from high school. By August of 1996, I was pregnant with my son, Keyon. This pregnancy was a horrible. The enemy fought me tooth and nail over Keyon.

I was abused mentally every day, "You shouldn't have this baby, how are you going to take care this baby, get an abortion, you can't even take care of yourself."

There were times I was afraid to go to sleep. I would hold my stomach to protect it. Four months into this pregnancy, I began to have contractions. It became a high-risk pregnancy and I was placed on bed rest. At six months, the contractions began again. My physician gave me shots in my side to help mature the baby's lungs. My son was determined to come into the world early, though.

After Keyon was born, he had problems breathing due to the medication they had given me. Before the doctors let me see Keyon, they informed me that he was born with yellow jaundice in his eyes and there may be a chance that he would not be able to see. It took a week to get an appointment with the eye specialist, but Keyon was able to see. His vision was bad, and he developed asthma, but God's grace covered them both!

The enemy desired to destroy both of my children! However, Keyon played basketball, he ran track, and exceled in football all throughout high school. Kaviona has developed into a beautiful young lady. I am so blessed by the gifts my children are to me. I thank God every day for protecting them from the enemy while I fought to get my life in order. I truly believe the scripture where God promises us He will never leave us nor forsake us (Hebrews 13:5).

"Even though I wasn't aware of His protective hand over us,
He was there with us all the time.
My beautiful children are a living testimony to that truth!"

I went through so much because of my disobedience and wanting to do things my way. I suffered being homeless so many times because I chose not to take responsibility for my poor decisions. I praise God because He was watching over me and my children even when I didn't know it at the time.

Growing up, I always sought the approval of those around me for everything. I always looked at what others wore and what others would say. I did not have an identity of my own, so I would shape my personality, style, or demeanor like those I saw around me. I really did not get an understanding of who I was until my children grew older.

Poor decisions and trying to be part of the crowd led me to have both of my children by the time I was eighteen. Not really understanding my responsibility and how I was going to provide for them, I suffered for many years trying to provide clothes, shoes, and a roof over their head. We moved over twenty times. I was trying to maintain the house, maintain my children, and keep my head above water working.

I was experiencing one of the lowest points of my life, though people around me had no idea that I was staying in a house with no water and no electric. I asked God why I was having to go through that until I realized it was a season to humble me and show me that I had to depend on Him. I stayed in the house for a week with no power and no running water. I would purchase several gallons of water daily to brush my teeth and flush the toilet. I would arrive at work around 6:00 a.m. so I could shower before anyone else arrived.

I will never forget when someone at work looked at me disgustedly and told me not to wear the shirt I had on again because it had a hole in it. That person had no idea that I was thankful to even have a shirt.

"That and many other experiences showed me that God will meet our needs even when we are in a place we brought about by our own poor choices and decisions."

> ***Even when we are too weak to have any faith left, he remains faithful to us and will help us,*** *for he cannot disown us who are part of himself, and he will always carry out his promises to us.* (2 Timothy 2:13 TLB emphasis added)

BOUND BY PAST DECISIONS

My advice to young women: *God has ordained a time and season to get married and have children. My past is my testimony to share and I would never change my past, therefore, if I can help the next one I will. Wait on God to give you a mate, someone who God has designed for you, someone that will be there for you, and pray with you through a storm. Wait for God to show you who you are in Him. Allow God to show you why He said you are fearfully and wonderfully made. Allow God to mold you into the person He has designed you to be. Go after your dreams and allow God to guide you so you can experience a truly full and prosperous life.*

Read and meditate on these verses from God's Word. Record in your journal what God reveals to you through each verse.

Psalm 139:14 says you are: ______________________________

____

1 Peter 2:4 says you are: ________________________________

____

Ephesians 2:10 says you are: _____________________________

____

Galatians 1:4 says you are: ______________________________

____

2 Peter 1:4 says you are: ________________________________

____

Read the Parable of the Prodigal Son Jesus told in Luke 15:11-32.

What poor decisions did this son make?

____

____

What were the consequences of his choices?

____

____

Have you made some poor decisions like this prodigal son?

____

____

Explain: ____

What was the response of the father when the son came to his senses and repented of his poor decisions?

____

____

How has this parable encouraged you in your relationship with your Heavenly Father?

____

____

Ask God to begin to reveal to you who He has designed you to be and what He wants you to do to begin to fulfill that divined destiny. Ask Him daily to guide your thoughts and your steps so you will stay true to His plan and His purpose for your life.

"When you become consumed by God's call on your life, everything will take on new meaning and significance. You will begin to see every facet of your life – including your pain – as a means through which God can work to bring others to Himself." – Charles Stanley[11]

[11] https://www.whatchristianswanttoknow.com/top-15-christian-quotes-about-pain-and-suffering/#ixzz57D3hHokO

CHAPTER 3

Bound by Hurt

"Past hurts and old injustices have a way of keeping us stuck in our tracks, unable to move forward or experience joy. The prospect of letting go forces us up against our three strongest emotional drivers: love, fear, and rage. It can take a radical reboot to get past yesterday." – Judith Sills Ph.D.[12]

"Years ago, I was calling on shut-ins," shares Dr. Larry Keefauver, pastoral psychologist and counselor. *"One woman, well into her eighties, particularly impressed me as a person of class and dignity. She spoke quietly with a demeanor that suggested either humility or perhaps abasement. For some indescribable reason, she seemed bound, overly reserved, completely strapped by some hidden force I could not adequately describe. Then I learned that for eighty years she had told no one of her guilt, shame, and her grief due to a childhood trauma. For decades, she had refused positions of leadership in the church, not because she did not have the potential nor the qualifications, but because she felt unworthy because of this shameful incident from her childhood. This woman of distinction, dignity, and class had never begun to reach her fullest potential because of a spirit*

---

[12] Judith Sills Ph.D. published on November 4, 2014 https://www.psychologytoday.com/articles/201411/let-it-go

of infirmity, a weakened and battered personality formed in a past trauma."[13]

There are people in every age who have experienced either physical or emotional trauma to such devastating proportions that their entire personalities are weakened. These traumatized people become prisoners of the past, seemingly helpless to escape. When we have been in prison long enough, when our past has bound us and paralyzed us for years, when either physical or emotional trauma has ravaged our spirits, then we find ourselves helpless. We become the victims of broken and battered spirits.

Howard Clinebell is probably the foremost authority on pastoral counseling in this country. He has written a book entitled, "Growth Counseling," where he writes, *"We human beings do not just have relationships. In a profound sense, we are our relationships. Our personalities are formed by the significant relationships of our childhood. We carry these relationships with us throughout our lives."*

The consequences of other people's choices affect us every day, and when those choices are major mistakes, they can affect our life in devastating ways. But no matter how other people have hurt us, God offers us hope that can empower us to overcome any circumstances.

"Before an eagle of God can really start to fly into the heights that God has in store for them in this life – that eagle has got to break off any chains that may be holding them back. These chains are keeping some of God's eagles grounded. And for

[13] Excerpt from "The Healing of Letting Go" by Dr. Larry Keefauver

many of God's eagles – some of these chains are things they are still holding onto from their past." – Michael Bradley[14]

My past hurt started when I was a child. I was in elementary school and my mom trusted someone to care for my sister and me. My mom believed it was safe, but it was there I was violated, not understanding what was going on. So many things happened to us as children that we were afraid to speak about. We did not realize that holding these things inside caused more harm than good. Our relationships were directly influenced by these childhood traumas.

Going through that experience as a child caused me to be over protective of my own children. It caused so much fear in me that I felt I had to keep them in my sight all the time. I was afraid to let them ride the school bus, go to the mall unattended, or spend the night at anyone's house.

Holding onto this past hurt and not dealing with it, caused me to try and cover up that hurt by being withdrawn. I built walls of protection around myself and was afraid to let anyone into a close relationship with me. I did not know what a healthy relationship was, so I avoided any and all relationships.

"For teens and adults who were abused as children, physical problems and emotional problems are closely interwoven," says Linda Luecken, PhD, an assistant professor of psychology at Arizona State University who has co-authored many studies on childhood trauma and stress. "Survivors of abuse may suffer from depression and low self-esteem, two conditions that can encourage risky behavior."

---

[14] Michael Bradley https://www.bible-knowledge.com/letting-go-of-your-past/

Carrying years of hurt and not talking about it caused me to act it out through a bad attitude and self-destructive behaviors. As a child, I was rude, selfish, backbiting, and ready to fight for any and all reasons. My attitude was horrible. This hurt from the past was always there in the back of my mind, taunting me, and building anger and bitterness in me like a volcano ready to explode.

When we read stories in the New Testament of how Jesus Christ heals and restores people, and sets them free to live life at its fullest, why do we hold on to those burdens from the past that keep us down? Why it is so hard for us to let go?

Dr. Larry Keefauver, pastoral psychologist and counselor, says, *"As I discussed a problem with a young woman I was counseling, she shared how*

she yelled at her two-year-old and often punished her child far beyond what was needed. When I asked her how she felt about that, she said, 'I feel very guilty, troubled, and upset because that's the way that my mother treated me and I don't want to treat my child like that, but I don't seem to be able to stop myself.' As we talked further, she admitted she felt resentment toward her mother for having treated her that way. When I asked her what she wanted to do about it, responded, "I want to tell my mother I resent her for the way she treated me as a child."

"At that moment," Dr. Keefauver says, *"There came an insight that she had not had before. The deeper problem was her resentment, bitterness, and even the guilt that she had for having those feelings toward her mother. At that point, I asked her what she wanted to do about it."*

"I want to tell my mom how I feel about her," she said. "Then I really want to tell her that I love her and that I forgive her."

For the first time since childhood, this young woman was released from her chains and set free by the grace of God.[15]

> *"One of the great things about life is that you can start over. With God there are always new beginnings and second chances. He specializes in giving people fresh starts. While you may feel overwhelmed at times and held back by painful recollections, haunting fears, remorse, shame, or guilt, God's power in your present life is not limited by what took place in your past. When you are governed and manipulated by your painful memories you allow your past to control your future. But when you choose to give God the controls, He can do amazing things with the rest of your life. You can start now and have a brand-new ending"* — Sue Augustine, When Your Past Is Hurting Your Present: Getting Beyond Fears That Hold You Back[16]

I never realized how bad all of this was, until I needed help and no one was there for me to turn to. In building my walls of protection around me, I had literally pushed everyone away. After begging someone to let me sleep on their sofa for the night until I could get to the bus station, I cried out to God.

The truth is all of us have needed to have our emotions healed by God. Each and every one of us knows emotional hurt. Either we have experience the hurt from outside that cuts deep into our emotions or we have experience the pain of having deep feelings that we are unable to express or release.

---

[15] Excerpt from "The Healing of Letting Go" by Dr. Larry Keefauver

[16] www.goodreads.com/work/quotes/752854-when-your-past-is-hurting-your-present-getting-beyond-fears-that-hold

Finally, I told God I was sorry for all the hateful things I had done and for not doing things His way. I reached out to Him and told Him I was ready to do things according to His plan. When I finally pushed through my past and touched the hem of His garment, that's when my healing really began!

> *And a woman who had suffered from a flow of blood for twelve years and had spent all her living upon physicians, and could not be healed by anyone, came up behind Him and touched the fringe of His garment, and immediately her flow of blood ceased. And Jesus said, Who is it who touched Me? When all were denying it, Peter and those who were with him said, Master, the multitudes surround You and press You on every side! But Jesus said, Someone did touch Me; for I perceived that [healing] power has gone forth from Me. And when the woman saw that she had not escaped notice, she came up trembling, and, falling down before Him, she declared in the presence of all the people for what reason she had touched Him and how she had been instantly cured. And He said to her, Daughter, your faith (your confidence and trust in Me) has made you well! Go enter into peace (untroubled, undisturbed well-being).* (Luke 8:43-48 AMPC)

The woman touched the Master's robe because she was desperate. Many people today are going through life in quiet desperation because they cannot find healing and peace for their hearts. The woman in Luke 8 touched the right person. People today try all sorts of self-help methods to find peace in their hearts and healing for their emotions. There are plenty of TV programs and books that people seek to find what they need. However, what they really need is Jesus. He is the right one to go to.

Whatever the cause of our desperation, there is hope and peace in Him. He invites us to come to Him, to touch Him, and find the peace and joy that we need. When the woman in the story touched Jesus, she was healed and made whole. Jesus is the answer to all our dilemmas and all that has us bound today.

So if the Son sets you free, you are truly free. (John 8:36 NLT)

BOUND BY PAST HURT

My advice to young women: *Hurt can mean bodily injury, bodily pain or mental or verbal hurt. Think back on things that have hurt you and use the scriptures provided below to help you overcome the hurt. It is time to truly be free so God can then use you to help free others from their past hurts.*

Psalm 34:18 says, "The Lord *is* near to those who have a broken heart, and saves such as have a contrite spirit."

2 Corinthians 1:3-4 says, "Blessed *be* the God and Father of our Lord Jesus Christ, the Father of mercies and God of all comfort, who comforts us in all our tribulation, that we may be able to comfort those who are in any trouble, with the comfort with which we ourselves are comforted by God."

Here Are Five Ways to Let Go of Past Hurts[17]

The only way you can accept new joy and happiness into your life is to make space for it.

1. **Make the decision to let it go.** Things do not disappear on their own. You need to make the commitment to "let it go." If you do not make this conscious choice up-front, you could end up self-sabotaging any effort to move on from this past hurt. Making the decision to let it go also means accepting you have a choice to let it go. To stop reliving the past pain, to stop going over the details of the story in your head every time you think of the other person (after you finish step 2 below).

2. **Express your pain — and your responsibility.** Express the pain the hurt made you feel, whether it is directly to the other person, or through just getting it out of your system (like venting to a friend, or writing in a journal, or writing a letter you never send to the other person). Get it all out of your system at once. Doing so will also help you understand what your hurt is about.

3. **Stop being the victim and blaming others.** In every moment, you have that choice — to continue to feel bad about another person's actions, or to *start feeling good*. You need to *take responsibility* for your own happiness, and not put such power into the hands of another person. Why would

[17] psychcentral.com/blog/learning-to-let-go-of-past

you let *the person who hurt you* — in the past — have such power, right here, right now?

4. **Focus on the present — the here and now — and joy.** When you focus on the here and now, you have less time to think about the past. When the past memories creep into your consciousness (as they are bound to do from time to time), acknowledge them for a moment and then bring yourself gently back into the present moment. Some people find it easier to do this with a conscious cue, such as saying to yourself, "It's alright. That was the past, and now I'm focused on my own happiness and doing ____________." Remember, if we crowd our brains and lives with hurt feelings, there is little room for anything positive. It's a *choice you're making* to continue to feel the hurt, rather than welcoming joy back into your life.

5. **Forgive them.** We may not have to forget another person's bad behaviors, but virtually everybody deserves our forgiveness. Sometimes we get stuck in our pain and our stubbornness, we can't even imagine forgiveness. Keep in mind that forgiveness is not saying, "I agree with what you did." Instead, it is saying, "I *don't agree* with what you did, but I forgive you anyway."

Forgiveness is not a sign of weakness, instead, it is simply saying, "I want to move forward in my life and welcome joy back into it. I can't do that fully until I let this go."

Forgive yourself is an important part of this step as well, as sometimes we may end up blaming ourselves for the situation or hurt. If you cannot forgive yourself, how will you be able to live in future peace and happiness?

The past is full of hurts, disappointments, failures, regrets, and people who have damaged our souls. Who really wants to carry all those reminders around day after day, year after year? No one, and yet we do it anyway.

> *"Letting go is one of the major cornerstones of being set free. Make a decision to release whatever is holding you back. Don't hang on to anything that is not empowering you to move forward. In reality, you always have the option of choosing whether you will focus on a hurtful past or fill your mind with uplifting thoughts of the present and all its blessings. Your mind cannot focus on both negative and positive ideas at the same time."*
> – Sue Augustine, When Your Past Is Hurting Your Present: Getting Beyond Fears That Hold You Back[18]

Focus on overcoming your past: Philippians 3:12-14 says, "Not that I have already attained, or am already perfected; but I press on, that I may lay hold of that for which Christ Jesus has also laid hold of me. Brethren, I do not count myself to have apprehended; but one thing *I do,* forgetting those things which are behind and reaching forward to those things which are ahead, I press toward the goal for the prize of the upward call of God in Christ Jesus" (NKJV).

Follow the instructions in Isaiah 43:18-19, which says, "Do not remember the former things, Nor consider the things of old.

[18] www.goodreads.com/work/quotes/752854-when-your-past-is-hurting-your-present-getting-beyond-fears-that-hold

Behold, I will do a new thing, Now it shall spring forth; Shall you not know it? I will even make a road in the wilderness and rivers in the desert" (NKJV).

Your words and thoughts are containers of power. They can carry in power from the Kingdom of God or the kingdom of darkness. You choose. This is one of your most powerful weapons against pulling down strongholds, because the Bible says out of the abundance of the heart the mouth speaks and also as a person thinks so they are. Change your thoughts and change your words and God's power will change your life.[19]

[19] Read more at http://www.beliefnet.com/faiths/galleries/10-steps-to-break-spiritual-strongholds.aspx?p=5#zG3Q4ylMHikSlA4Q.99

CHAPTER 4

Bound by "My Mind"

For God has not given us a spirit of fear, but of power and of love and of a sound mind. (2 Timothy 1:7)

The mind is defined as the element, part, substance, or process that reasons, thinks, feels, wills, perceives, and judges.[20] If the enemy of your soul can keep you confused by how **you feel**, how **you see** things, and who **he desires you** to be, he has **you bound**. I have firsthand experience in what this can mean when you give the enemy a foothold in your mind.

At fifteen, I had no understanding that the road before me would leave me homeless, broken hearted, searching for love in all the wrong places, losing everything, attempting suicide, spending a night in jail, losing my mother, my father forsaking me, and being a single parent. One decision I made based on fear pushed me outside the will of God and caused me to suffer much needless pain and hurt.

During my pregnancy with Keyon, I was **afraid** to tell my dad. I went through the entire pregnancy without seeing him. Finally, when Keyon was three months old, we went to go see my dad.

We showed up at his door and he asked, "Who is this little boy?"

---

[20] http://www.dictionary.com/browse/mind

I told him, "This is Keyon, my son."

Keyon began to laugh and my dad embraced him, totally smitten by his grandson.

My fear had been unfounded, but it kept me and my son from a relationship with my dad.

Unfortunately, I had not yet learned my lesson and continued making decisions based on fear and the confusion in my mind. Keyon was four months when I found out I was two months pregnant. I did not seek God's guidance or even the counsel of godly mentors. After a hard decision, I chose to have an abortion.

Knowing what I know now and the pain I endured mentally and physically from making that choice, I wouldn't have made that decision. I have since repented and asked God for forgiveness and He has forgiven me. However, I still live with the consequences of that decision. Please allow God to guide you through and do things God's way. It took years to bounce back mentally from the abortion. I had given the devil a foothold in my mind and he continued to cause confusion and fear to motivate my decisions and my actions for many years afterwards.

> *For God is not the author of confusion but of peace.* (1 Corinthians 14:33 NKJV)

During the next two years, my relationship with the man I was living with went steadily downhill. Our relationship was over, but I did not want to admit that it was. I began drinking and partying all night without him. While he worked during the day, I slept and took care of Kaviona and Keyon. I remember feeling so depressed and sad that one day I had a bottle of pills and began taking them. He came up behind me and made me spit them up. Suicide was a constant thought. Even if I did not try it, I would write about it in my journals. The enemy was feeding my mind with suicidal thoughts.

"The Bible warns us that thoughts are a powerful force in our life. Romans 12:2 says the only way to keep from conforming to the values and morals of the world is through constantly renewing our minds by seeking to know God's will for our lives."

Since I did not embrace this truth, Kaviona and Keyon saw more fussing and fighting during these two years than the rest of their young lives. Every time I would leave them to go out, they would scream and yell. I would cover up the hurt, pain, and disappointment in my life with drinking and fighting in the streets. I thank God for grace and mercy or I would never have survived this destructive time in my life.

There is one fight that stands out above the rest that shows just how out of control my mind was at this time in my life. It was when we were in Myrtle Beach, South Carolina. A girl and two guys in another car almost caused us to hit a utility pole. In a fit of road rage, we went after them. I jumped out of our car and started cussing. I struck one of the guys in the face. He hit me back and my nose began to bleed. I just went after him like a wild cat. I wore his head out punching and scratching him. The next thing I knew, a friend rammed her four-inch heel right into his forehead. Blood began to run down his face and into his eyes. We were all fighting and yelling and causing such a scene that people began to stop and watch. The girl and the two guys finally gave up and ran to get into their car. We drove off after them, but by God's grace, we lost them in traffic. It's a wonder we weren't all killed as a result of our foolish, anger filled actions.

> *"Be angry and do not sin": do not let the sun go down on your wrath, nor give place to the devil.* (Ephesians 4:26-27 NKJV)

My advice to young people is to be aware that the enemy will have you focused on what is going on right now and not on the repercussions and consequences of your choices in the future. I was not looking or thinking about God's plan for my life or my family. I had no idea the enemy did not want me to make it, and that if I stayed on the path he had laid out for me I would spend eternity in hell.

I put my trust in things and people instead of understanding that only God has promised to never leave me. I was dependent on my job instead of understanding that God promised to supply all my needs. I tried to figure out how to make ends meet instead of understanding that God knows the beginning and the end and has a plan for me to prosper. I even tried to battle with the devil on my own instead of understanding that no weapon formed against me shall prosper because Jesus has already gained the victory.

I was convinced I was a loser and always would be. I was so confused in my mind that I self-medicated myself against the pain and disappointment in my life with alcohol. I was ready to give up on myself and my life. I am so thankful God never gave up on me.

> *For He Himself has said, "**I will never leave you nor forsake you.**"* (Hebrews 13:5 NKJV emphasis added)

BOUND BY "MY MIND"

You are complete in Him, who is the head of all principality and power. (Colossians 2:10 NKJV)

"I put my trust in things and people instead of understanding that only God has promised to never leave me."

What have you put your trust in instead of God?

____

____

____

What does Proverbs 3:5-6 say about putting your trust in God?

____

____

____

"I was dependent on my job instead of understanding that my God promised to supply all my needs."

Have you been dependent on an employer instead of God?

____

____

____

"I tried to figure out how to make ends meet instead of understanding that God knows the beginning and the end and has a plan for me to prosper."

Can you predict the future? Do you know the end from the beginning? Who does?

____

____

____

"I even tried to do battle with the devil on my own instead of understanding that no weapon formed against me shall prosper because Jesus has already gained the victory."

If you have been trying to battle the devil on your own, how is that working out for you?

____

____

____

Seek the Lord and follow His plan. If you are not sure what His plan is, pray and stand still until He answers you. Do not be afraid to seek godly counsel, but make sure God confirms it as well.

Read Romans 12:2. How can you keep from allowing the devil access to your mind?

____

____

____

Read Ephesians 4:26-27. Why is important to control your anger?

____

____

____

Read Ephesians 6:10-18. Study the weapons God has given you to do battle with the devil with Him instead of on your own. List each piece of the armor of God and how to use it.

Record in your journal the victories you achieve as you acknowledge God in all of your ways and use the tools and weapons He has given you so you are no longer bound by your mind.

"Let God have your life; He can do more with it than you can."

– Dwight L. Moody[21]

[21] https://www.christianquotes.info/top-quotes/16-awesome-quotes-about-surrendering-to-god/#ixzz57DHhdglr

CONCLUSION

Surrendering My Life to Christ

January 2003: The last three months of my mom's life, I spent as much time with her as possible. Even though I did not know how sick she was, God positioned me to spend more time with her during her final days. He allowed our relationship to mend as I accompanied her on doctors' appointments, dialysis appointments, and getting her medications. We had to shave all her hair off due to the medical treatment.

My last Christmas with her was different. My sisters and I began to argue as usual, but this time she responded differently.

She gazed at us and said, "When I close my eyes, ya'll better get along."

We looked at her not understanding she would die the following month. Three days before my mom passed away, we went to the Emergency Room. I stayed with her all-night long. The next day we talked and laughed. Mom just seemed to be at peace. I talked with her about planning her next birthday party. I walked out the room and when I came back, my mom had one hand raised up and she was looking up to the ceiling. I asked her if she was okay. She had a peaceful look on her face. Looking back, I truly believe my mom was talking with God.

The following day, a specialist told her she would have to have the Intravenous (IV) grafted into her arm due to her veins collapsing.

My mom told me not to allow them to do the procedure. She said she was tired and had gone through enough.

I did not understand that the last three months of her life was a time of restoration in our relationship. God used that time to restore the love I had for my mom. I realized it had been many years since I had told her, "I love you, Mom."

On one morning, as I was helping her with her medications, I said, "Mom, I love you."

She smiled and hugged me. I felt that moment was when our relationship was fully restored and I thank God for the opportunity He gave me.

As long as God continues to breathe His breathe into my lungs, I will tell people everywhere, "Tomorrow is not promised. Love your mom and work out the differences with her. Once she's gone, that's it."

I missed out on so much because of hatred, bitterness, and deceit from the enemy. Value your mom, her words of wisdom, respect her, and pray for her. I am thankful to God for allowing me that time with her. The last time I saw my mom, she was on life support. My grandmother had called us to the hospital and told my sister, Robin and me it had been twenty-four hours since mom had responded. She told us we had to decide whether to keep her on life support or take her off. After they pulled the cord, I knew she was gone–her hand was cold. I could feel my heart drop.

During that time, the enemy talked to me and made me believe that I should be with my mom. The enemy would give me dreams of my mom dressed in white and telling me to come with her. I learned that the enemy picks an opportune time to creep in and if it was not for my best friend, Malia, I might have acted and actually taken my life.

There was point in my life that I was so depressed, full of grief, and wounded that I had made up my mind I was done helping people, I was done cleaning the church, I was done preaching, I was done teaching, I was done picking people up, and I was done doing anything related to church. I had been faithful in all of those things, but, I was dealing with church hurt.

I was invited and agreed to go to visit Victorious Life of Faith Church in District Heights, Maryland, but in my mind I was thinking, *If one person says anything I don't like, we're leaving!* The usher, the greeter, and the lady next to me were all very nice. Pastor Victor Furr preached about Jeremiah that day.

At the conclusion of his message, Pastor Furr said, "Somebody told God, 'I'm not cleaning, I'm not picking anyone up, and I'm not doing anything.' But God told me to tell you that you're coming out of retirement."

My mouth dropped. I received a note from my daughter that said, "Mom, God is talking to you!"

God was indeed talking to me directly. I could not deny it.

I stayed under Pastor Furr's leadership for the next year. That year gave me time to focus, heal, spend time with God, and really decide if I was ready to commit to another ministry.

I can honestly say that surrendering to God is a life time process. We may think we have it altogether, but the secret is to completely surrender to God on a daily basis. That is because no matter who we are, we will face daily battles. God desires for us to be free in our thoughts, life patterns, our hearts, and free from the things that are behind us.

Surrendering My Life to Christ

> *You are complete in Him, who is the head of all principality and power.* (Colossians 2:10 NKJV)

There was a time in my life when I was so empty that I sought the approval of everyone around me. However, when I truly understood Colossians 2:10, I understood that I am complete in Christ. No new car, no new house, no man, or a connection with any other person would complete me or give me what I desired. It took me so long to realize that the only way I could truly feel complete was to totally surrender my heart, my life, and my plans to Christ. The only way I could be completely whole was through a relationship with Jesus. Jesus uses our faith to bring total healing and wholeness to our lives. His healing power goes deep within us and brings about physical, emotional, and spiritual healing and wholeness.

Surrender means to yield to the possession or power of another; deliver up possession of on demand or under duress.[22] The Bible is full of examples of those who surrendered immediately and those who fought the process. I was one who fought the process, but I pray you have learned from my mistakes and will use the scriptures provided to surrender your heart and goals to Christ.

For the next thirty days, choose one scripture from the list below. Look it up in various translations of the Bible. Study it, meditate on it, and ask the Lord to give you insight into what it means to you and your life situation. This process will help you gain a closer relationship with God and give you a clearer perception of His great love and plan for your life.

The most powerful thing you will ever have is your ability to choose. God has given us a mind to choose. How will you choose to live the rest of your life?

---

[22] https://www.merriam-webster.com/dictionary/surrender

Day 1: Read 1 Corinthians 2:16. J. B. Phillips says, *"But the unspiritual man simply cannot accept the matters which the Spirit deals with—they just don't make sense to him, for, after all, you must be spiritual to see spiritual things. The spiritual man, on the other hand, has an insight into the meaning of everything, though his insight may baffle the man of the world. This is because the former is sharing in God's wisdom, and 'Who has known the mind of the Lord that he may instruct him?' Incredible as it may sound, we who are spiritual have the very thoughts of Christ!"*[23]

Record in your journal the insight the Lord has given you as to what it means to you and your life situation. How has this helped you gain a closer relationship with God and given you a clearer perception of His great love and plan for your life? How will you choose to live the rest of your life?

____

____

____

Thank your loving heavenly Father for the amazing insights He has given you today to be able to move from being bound by the hurt and pain from your past into a life of prosperity and power.

Day 2: Read Joshua 24:15. *The Amplified Bible says, "If it is unacceptable in your sight to serve the LORD, choose for yourselves this day whom you will serve: whether the gods which your fathers served that were on the other side of the River, or the gods of the*

[23] J.B. Phillips New Testament in Modern English by J.B Phillips copyright © 1960, 1972 J. B. Phillips. Administered by The Archbishops' Council of the Church of England. Used by Permission.

Amorites in whose land you live; but as for me and my house, we will serve the LORD."

Record in your journal the insight the Lord has given you as to what it means to you and your life situation. How has this helped you gain a closer relationship with God and given you a clearer perception of His great love and plan for your life? How will you choose to live the rest of your life?

Declare today that you have chosen to serve the Lord. Thank Him for His great love for you and for the healing He is doing in your heart and mind.

Day 3: Read Romans 12:2. *The New Living Translation says, "Don't copy the behavior and customs of this world, but let God transform you into a new person by changing the way you think. Then you will learn to know God's will for you, which is good and pleasing and perfect."*

Record in your journal the insight the Lord has given you as to what it means to you and your life situation. How has this helped you gain a closer relationship with God and given you a clearer perception of His great love and plan for your life? How will you choose to live the rest of your life?

Thank your loving heavenly Father for the strength to live your life His way. Ask His continual help in transforming your thinking so you are not pulled into copying the behavior of this world. Thank Him for showing you His perfect will for your life today.

Day 4: Read Ephesians 4:23. *The Amplified Bible says, "And be constantly renewed in the spirit of your mind [having a fresh mental and spiritual attitude]."*

Record in your journal the insight the Lord has given you as to what it means to you and your life situation. How has this helped you gain a closer relationship with God and given you a clearer perception of His great love and plan for your life? How will you choose to live the rest of your life?

____

____

____

Thank the Lord today as He renews your mind and gives you a clear and fresh perspective and a brand new attitude toward the wonderful work He is doing in your mind to free you from the hurts of the past.

Day 5: Read Colossians 3:2. *The Message Bible says, "So if you're serious about living this new resurrection life with Christ, act like it. Pursue the things over which Christ presides. Don't shuffle along, eyes to the ground, absorbed with the things right in front of you.*

Look up, and be alert to what is going on around Christ—that's where the action is. See things from his perspective."[24]

Record in your journal the insight the Lord has given you as to what it means to you and your life situation. How has this helped you gain a closer relationship with God and given you a clearer perception of His great love and plan for your life? How will you choose to live the rest of your life?

___

___

___

Thank Jesus today for eyes to see things from His perspective and the strength to choose to live your life in the power of His resurrection. Ask Him to help you be more alert to what He is doing in your life as He moves you from bound to found.

Day 6: Read 2 Timothy 1:7. *The Amplified Bible says, "For God did not give us a spirit of timidity or cowardice or fear, but [He has given us a spirit] of power and of love and of sound judgment and personal discipline [abilities that result in a calm, well-balanced mind and self-control]."*

Record in your journal the insight the Lord has given you as to what it means to you and your life situation. How has this helped you gain a closer relationship with God and given you a clearer perception

[24] The Message **(MSG)** Copyright © 1993, 1994, 1995, 1996, 2000, 2001, 2002 by Eugene H. Peterson.

of His great love and plan for your life? How will you choose to live the rest of your life?

____

____

____

Thank God that He has given you a calm, well-balanced mind. Thank Him for strengthening your personal discipline and giving you the sound judgment you need to walk in power and love today instead of fear.

Day 7: Read John 10:10. *The Amplified Bible says, "The thief comes only in order to steal and kill and destroy. I came that they may have and enjoy life, and have it in abundance [to the full, till it overflows]."*

Record in your journal the insight the Lord has given you as to what it means to you and your life situation. How has this helped you gain a closer relationship with God and given you a clearer perception of His great love and plan for your life? How will you choose to live the rest of your life?

____

____

____

Thank Jesus for coming to bring you an abundant, full, joy-filled life and for helping you to stand against the thief who has tried to steal your peace and joy. Declare your victory over this thief today in Jesus' name.

Day 8: Read Matthew 6:33. *The Amplified Bible says, "But first and most importantly seek (aim at, strive after) His kingdom and His righteousness [His way of doing and being right—the attitude and character of God], and all these things will be given to you also."*

Record in your journal the insight the Lord has given you as to what it means to you and your life situation. How has this helped you gain a closer relationship with God and given you a clearer perception of His great love and plan for your life? How will you choose to live the rest of your life?

____

____

____

Declare that you are seeking His kingdom and choosing His way of doing things. Thank Him that today your life will reflect His kingdom in all that you say and do. Thank Him for providing all that you need today to live a life of godliness and power.

Day 9: Read John 16:33. *The Message Bible says, "I've told you all this so that trusting me, you will be unshakable and assured, deeply at peace. In this godless world you will continue to experience difficulties. But take heart! I've conquered the world."*[25]

Record in your journal the insight the Lord has given you as to what it means to you and your life situation. How has this helped you gain a closer relationship with God and given you a clearer perception

[25] The Message **(MSG)** Copyright © 1993, 1994, 1995, 1996, 2000, 2001, 2002 by Eugene H. Peterson.

of His great love and plan for your life? How will you choose to live the rest of your life?

Declare you have chosen to trust the Lord no matter what difficulties you might experience in this godless world as you go about your daily activities today. When the enemy tries to steal your peace, remind him that God's Word says Jesus has already conquered the world!

Day 10: Read Proverbs 23:7. *The New King James Bible says, "For as he thinks in his heart, so is he."*

Record in your journal the insight the Lord has given you as to what it means to you and your life situation. How has this helped you gain a closer relationship with God and given you a clearer perception of His great love and plan for your life? How will you choose to live the rest of your life?

Thank the Lord that He has given you His Word and as you fill your mind and heart with His promises and assurances, you are being transformed into His new creation.

Day 11: Read Romans 8:31. *The Message Bible says, "So, what do you think? With God on our side like this, how can we lose?"*[26]

[26] The Message (MSG) Copyright © 1993, 1994, 1995, 1996, 2000, 2001, 2002 by Eugene H. Peterson.

Record in your journal the insight the Lord has given you as to what it means to you and your life situation. How has this helped you gain a closer relationship with God and given you a clearer perception of His great love and plan for your life? How will you choose to live the rest of your life?

____

____

____

Thank your loving heavenly Father for defending you against any and all attacks that might come at you today. Continually declare that with God on your side, you have the victory over what has had you bound.

Day 12: Read Isaiah 54:17. *The Amplified Bible says, "No weapon that is formed against you will succeed; And every tongue that rises against you in judgment you will condemn. This [peace, righteousness, security, and triumph over opposition] is the heritage of the servants of the LORD, and this is their vindication from Me," says the LORD.* [27]

Record in your journal the insight the Lord has given you as to what it means to you and your life situation. How has this helped you gain a closer relationship with God and given you a clearer perception of His great love and plan for your life? How will you choose to live the rest of your life?

____

____

____

[27] The Message (MSG) Copyright © 1993, 1994, 1995, 1996, 2000, 2001, 2002 by Eugene H. Peterson.

Thank the Lord for this powerful heritage He has given you. Thank Him and declare His truth that no weapon formed against you will succeed and no tongue can come against you in judgment. Thank the Lord for His peace, security, and triumph over every opposition as you choose to serve Him with your life today.

Day 13: Read 1 Corinthians 10:13. *The Amplified Bible says, "For no temptation (no trial regarded as enticing to sin), [no matter how it comes or where it leads] has overtaken you and laid hold on you that is not common to man [that is, no temptation or trial has come to you that is beyond human resistance and that is not adjusted and adapted and belonging to human experience, and such as man can bear]. But God is faithful [to His Word and to His compassionate nature], and He [can be trusted] not to let you be tempted and tried and assayed beyond your ability and strength of resistance and power to endure, but with the temptation He will [always] also provide the way out (the means of escape to a landing place), that you may be capable and strong and powerful to bear up under it patiently."* [28]

Record in your journal the insight the Lord has given you as to what it means to you and your life situation. How has this helped you gain a closer relationship with God and given you a clearer perception of His great love and plan for your life? How will you choose to live the rest of your life?

____

____

____

[28] The Message (MSG) Copyright © 1993, 1994, 1995, 1996, 2000, 2001, 2002 by Eugene H. Peterson.

Thank the Lord today for His powerful promises to give you the ability, power, and strength to resist the temptation to allow your past to keep you bound. Thank Him for His faithfulness and the victory over every trial you may face as you choose to trust Him to guide you through to your "landing place."

Day 14: Read Proverbs 3:5-6. *The Message Bible says, "Trust GOD from the bottom of your heart; don't try to figure out everything on your own. Listen for GOD's voice in everything you do, everywhere you go; he's the one who will keep you on track. Don't assume that you know it all. Run to GOD! Run from evil! Your body will glow with health, your very bones will vibrate with life! Honor GOD with everything you own; give him the first and the best. Your barns will burst, your wine vats will brim over. But don't, dear friend, resent GOD's discipline; don't sulk under his loving correction. It's the child he loves that GOD corrects; a father's delight is behind all this."*[29]

Record in your journal the insight the Lord has given you as to what it means to you and your life situation. How has this helped you gain a closer relationship with God and given you a clearer perception of His great love and plan for your life? How will you choose to live the rest of your life?

____

____

____

[29] The Message **(MSG)** Copyright © 1993, 1994, 1995, 1996, 2000, 2001, 2002 by Eugene H. Peterson.

Thank the Lord that you do not have to figure things out for yourself. Thank Him that He is with you everywhere you go and has the answer to everything you will have to deal with today. Ask Him to keep you on track all throughout your day and rejoice in His provision as you seek to hear His voice.

Day 15: Read John 8:32. *The Message Bible says, "Then Jesus turned to the Jews who had claimed to believe in him. "If you stick with this, living out what I tell you, you are my disciples for sure. Then you will experience for yourselves the truth, and the truth will free you."*[30]

Record in your journal the insight the Lord has given you as to what it means to you and your life situation. How has this helped you gain a closer relationship with God and given you a clearer perception of His great love and plan for your life? How will you choose to live the rest of your life?

____

____

____

Thank the Lord that as you choose to live your life as His disciple, you will discover the truth about who He says you are and experience the freedom from what has kept you bound.

Day 16: Read 2 Corinthians 10:5. *The Message Bible says, "The world is unprincipled. It's dog-eat-dog out there! The world doesn't fight fair. But we don't live or fight our battles that way—never have and never*

[30] The Message **(MSG)** Copyright © 1993, 1994, 1995, 1996, 2000, 2001, 2002 by Eugene H. Peterson.

will. The tools of our trade aren't for marketing or manipulation, but they are for demolishing that entire massively corrupt culture. We use our powerful God-tools for smashing warped philosophies, tearing down barriers erected against the truth of God, fitting every loose thought and emotion and impulse into the structure of life shaped by Christ. Our tools are ready at hand for clearing the ground of every obstruction and building lives of obedience into maturity."[31]

Record in your journal the insight the Lord has given you as to what it means to you and your life situation. How has this helped you gain a closer relationship with God and given you a clearer perception of His great love and plan for your life? How will you choose to live the rest of your life?

___

___

___

Thank the Lord today for the powerful God-tools He has given you to deal with every lie, thought, emotion, and impulse that has kept you bound and obstructed you from a life of obedience to Him.

Day 17: Read Philippians 2:5-8. *The Message Bible says, "Think of yourselves the way Christ Jesus thought of himself. He had equal status with God but didn't think so much of himself that he had to cling to the advantages of that status no matter what. Not at all. When the time came, he set aside the privileges of deity and took on the status of a slave, became human! Having become human, he stayed human.*

[31] The Message **(MSG)** Copyright © 1993, 1994, 1995, 1996, 2000, 2001, 2002 by Eugene H. Peterson.

It was an incredibly humbling process. He didn't claim special privileges. Instead, he lived a selfless, obedient life and then died a selfless, obedient death—and the worst kind of death at that—a crucifixion."[32]

Record in your journal the insight the Lord has given you as to what it means to you and your life situation. How has this helped you gain a closer relationship with God and given you a clearer perception of His great love and plan for your life? How will you choose to live the rest of your life?

Thank Jesus today for the amazing choice He made so that you can live free from the powers of darkness that threaten to overtake you and keep you bound to your past.

Day 18: Read Romans 9:33. *The Amplified Bible says, "As it is written, Behold I am laying in Zion a Stone that will make men stumble, a Rock that will make them fall; but he who believes in Him [who adheres to, trusts in, and relies on Him] shall not be put to shame nor be disappointed in his expectations."*[33]

Record in your journal the insight the Lord has given you as to what it means to you and your life situation. How has this helped you gain

[32] The Message **(MSG)** Copyright © 1993, 1994, 1995, 1996, 2000, 2001, 2002 by Eugene H. Peterson.

[33] The Message (MSG) Copyright © 1993, 1994, 1995, 1996, 2000, 2001, 2002 by Eugene H. Peterson.

a closer relationship with God and given you a clearer perception of His great love and plan for your life? How will you choose to live the rest of your life?

____

____

____

Thank the Lord today that as you put your trust in Him and in His promises, you no longer have to be bound by shame or disappointment.

Day 19: Read Acts 17:28. *The Amplified Bible says, "For in Him we live and move and exist [that is, in Him we actually have our being], as even some of your own poets have said, 'For we also are His children.'"*[34]

Record in your journal the insight the Lord has given you as to what it means to you and your life situation. How has this helped you gain a closer relationship with God and given you a clearer perception of His great love and plan for your life? How will you choose to live the rest of your life?

____

____

____

Thank your heavenly Father that you are officially part of His family. Thank Him that you are His child and can go to Him whenever the things of your past try to confuse you. Thank Him that His loving

[34] The Message (MSG) Copyright © 1993, 1994, 1995, 1996, 2000, 2001, 2002 by Eugene H. Peterson.

arms are always inviting you to come and sit in His lap and share your innermost feelings with Him.

Day 20: Read Colossians 3:1. *The Amplified Bible says, "If then you have been raised with Christ [to a new life, thus sharing His resurrection from the dead], aim at and seek the [rich, eternal treasures] that are above, where Christ is, seated at the right hand of God."*[35]

Record in your journal the insight the Lord has given you as to what it means to you and your life situation. How has this helped you gain a closer relationship with God and given you a clearer perception of His great love and plan for your life? How will you choose to live the rest of your life?

____

____

____

Thank the Lord today for the new life you have in Him. Thank Him for how this powerful new life has released you from the bondage of your past, your fear, and your unwise decisions.

Day 21: Read 2 Peter 1:4. *J.B. Phillips says, "He has by his own action given us everything that is necessary for living the truly good life, in allowing us to know the one who has called us to him, through his own glorious goodness. It is through him that God's greatest and most precious promises have become available to us men, making*

[35] The Message (MSG) Copyright © 1993, 1994, 1995, 1996, 2000, 2001, 2002 by Eugene H. Peterson.

it possible for you to escape the inevitable disintegration that lust produces in the world and to share in God's essential nature."[36]

Record in your journal the insight the Lord has given you as to what it means to you and your life situation. How has this helped you gain a closer relationship with God and given you a clearer perception of His great love and plan for your life? How will you choose to live the rest of your life?

____

____

____

Thank the Lord Jesus for giving you everything that is necessary for living the truly godly life. Thank Him for giving you access to God's greatest and most precious promises. Thank Him for making it possible for you to escape the bondages of the past so you can walk in the new life He has purposed for you.

Day 22: Read Galatians 1:4. *The Amplified Bible says, "Who gave (yielded) Himself up [to atone] for our sins [and to save and sanctify us], in order to rescue and deliver us from this present wicked age and world order, in accordance with the will and purpose and plan of our God and Father."*[37]

---

[36] J.B. Phillips New Testament in Modern English by J.B Phillips copyright © 1960, 1972 J. B. Phillips. Administered by The Archbishops' Council of the Church of England. Used by Permission.

[37] The Message (MSG) Copyright © 1993, 1994, 1995, 1996, 2000, 2001, 2002 by Eugene H. Peterson.

Record in your journal the insight the Lord has given you as to what it means to you and your life situation. How has this helped you gain a closer relationship with God and given you a clearer perception of His great love and plan for your life? How will you choose to live the rest of your life?

___

___

___

Thank the Lord for rescuing and delivering you from all that has bound you and for how He has prepared you to fulfill the purpose and plan of God for your life through His loving sacrifice.

Day 23: Read Jeremiah 29:11. *The New International Reader's Bible says, "I know the plans I have for you," announces the Lord. "I want you to enjoy success. I do not plan to harm you. I will give you hope for the years to come."*[38]

Record in your journal the insight the Lord has given you as to what it means to you and your life situation. How has this helped you gain a closer relationship with God and given you a clearer perception of His great love and plan for your life? How will you choose to live the rest of your life?

___

___

___

[38] New International Reader's Version (NIRV) Copyright © 1995, 1996, 1998, 2014 by Biblica, Inc.®. Used by permission

Thank the Lord that He truly does have a specific set of plans for your life. Thank Him for the hope He has given you for the years to come. Ask Him to guide you through each day toward the fulfillment of those plans.

Day 24: Read 1 Peter 2:4. *J.B. Phillips says, "You come to him, as living stones to the immensely valuable living stone (which men rejected but God chose), to be built up into a spiritual House of God, in which you, like holy priests, can offer those spiritual sacrifices which are acceptable to God by Jesus Christ. There is a passage to this effect in scripture, and it runs like this: 'Behold, I lay in Zion a chief cornerstone, elect, precious, and he who believes on him will by no means be put to shame'."*[39]

Record in your journal the insight the Lord has given you as to what it means to you and your life situation. How has this helped you gain a closer relationship with God and given you a clearer perception of His great love and plan for your life? How will you choose to live the rest of your life?

____

____

____

Declare today that you will not reject the amazing sacrifice and the shame the Lord Jesus endured so that you would by no means be put to shame. Whenever the enemy tries to fill you with shame from your past, remind him you believe in and serve the Living God.

[39] J.B. Phillips New Testament in Modern English by J.B Phillips copyright © 1960, 1972 J. B. Phillips. Administered by The Archbishops' Council of the Church of England. Used by Permission.

Day 25: Read Romans 8:28. *The New Living Translation of the Bible says, "And we know that God causes everything to work together for the good of those who love God and are called according to his purpose for them."* [40]

Record in your journal the insight the Lord has given you as to what it means to you and your life situation. How has this helped you gain a closer relationship with God and given you a clearer perception of His great love and plan for your life? How will you choose to live the rest of your life?

____

____

____

Thank your loving heavenly Father for working out everything that happens in your life for good. Declare your love for Him today and thank Him for moving you forward toward His plan and purpose for your life as He turns what the enemy meant for evil into good.

Day 26: Read James 1:2-8. *The J.B. Phillips New Testament in Modern English says, "The Christian can even welcome trouble. When all kinds of trials and temptations crowd into your lives my brothers, don't resent them as intruders, but welcome them as friends! Realize that they come to test your faith and to produce in you the quality of endurance. But let the process go on until that endurance is fully developed, and you will find you have become men of mature character with the right sort of independence. And if, in the process, any*

[40] The Message (MSG) Copyright © 1993, 1994, 1995, 1996, 2000, 2001, 2002 by Eugene H. Peterson.

of you does not know how to meet any particular problem he has only to ask God—who gives generously to all men without making them feel foolish or guilty—and he may be quite sure that the necessary wisdom will be given him. But he must ask in sincere faith without secret doubts as to whether he really wants God's help or not. The man who trusts God, but with inward reservations, is like a wave of the sea, carried forward by the wind one moment and driven back the next. That sort of man cannot hope to receive anything from God, and the life of a man of divided loyalty will reveal instability at every turn."[41]

Record in your journal the insight the Lord has given you as to what it means to you and your life situation. How has this helped you gain a closer relationship with God and given you a clearer perception of His great love and plan for your life? How will you choose to live the rest of your life?

____

____

____

Thank God that whatever trial or problem you are called to face today, you can go to Him and ask for the wisdom to handle it His way. Thank Him that you no longer have to be carried through life on waves of doubt and fear because you are secure in your faith in Him.

Day 27: Read Ephesians 4:26-27. *The Amplified Bible says, "Be angry [at sin—at immorality, at injustice, at ungodly behavior], yet do not*

[41] J.B. Phillips New Testament in Modern English by J.B Phillips copyright © 1960, 1972 J. B. Phillips. Administered by The Archbishops' Council of the Church of England. Used by Permission.

sin; do not let your anger [cause you shame, nor allow it to] last until the sun goes down. And do not give the devil an opportunity [to lead you into sin by holding a grudge, or nurturing anger, or harboring resentment, or cultivating bitterness]." [42]

Record in your journal the insight the Lord has given you as to what it means to you and your life situation. How has this helped you gain a closer relationship with God and given you a clearer perception of His great love and plan for your life? How will you choose to live the rest of your life?

____

____

____

Thank God that you are no longer bound by the anger, resentment, and bitterness the devil has tried to incite within you over events in your past. Thank Him for the power He has given you to forgive those who have hurt you in the past so the enemy no longer has a foothold in your life.

Day 28: Read Psalm 139:14. *The Message Bible says, "Oh yes, you shaped me first inside, then out; you formed me in my mother's womb. I thank you, High God—you're breathtaking! Body and soul, I am marvelously made! I worship in adoration—what a creation! You know me inside and out, you know every bone in my body; You know exactly how I was made, bit by bit, how I was sculpted from nothing into something. Like an open book, you watched me grow from conception*

[42] The Message (MSG) Copyright © 1993, 1994, 1995, 1996, 2000, 2001, 2002 by Eugene H. Peterson.

to birth; all the stages of my life were spread out before you, The days of my life all prepared before I'd even lived one day."[43]

Record in your journal the insight the Lord has given you as to what it means to you and your life situation. How has this helped you gain a closer relationship with God and given you a clearer perception of His great love and plan for your life? How will you choose to live the rest of your life?

____

____

____

No matter what the world tries to tell you, thank God that you are His masterpiece. Thank Him for how He made you and formed you and sculpted you in your mother's womb. Thank Him for who He has created you to be as His beloved child.

Day 29: Read Luke 10:19. *The Passion Translation of the Bible says, "Now you understand that I have imparted to you all my authority to trample over his kingdom. You will trample upon every demon before you and overcome every power Satan possesses. Absolutely nothing will be able to harm you as you walk in this authority."*[44]

Record in your journal the insight the Lord has given you as to what it means to you and your life situation. How has this helped you gain

[43] The Message (MSG) Copyright © 1993, 1994, 1995, 1996, 2000, 2001, 2002 by Eugene H. Peterson.

[44] The Passion Translation (TPT) The Passion Translation®. Copyright © 2017 by BroadStreet Publishing® Group, LLC. Used by permission. All rights reserved. thePassionTranslation.com

a closer relationship with God and given you a clearer perception of His great love and plan for your life? How will you choose to live the rest of your life?

____

____

____

Thank the Lord for the amazing authority He has given you to trample upon **everything** the devil sends to try to take you out and keep you from fulfilling God's plan and purpose in your life. Thank Him for the promise that nothing will be able to stand against you when you stand in His power and authority. Declare that every chain that has kept you bound has been broken in the authority you have in Jesus' name.

Day 30: Read Psalm 34:18. *The Living Bible says, "The Lord is close to those whose hearts are breaking; he rescues those who are humbly sorry for their sins."*[45]

Record in your journal the insight the Lord has given you as to what it means to you and your life situation. How has this helped you gain a closer relationship with God and given you a clearer perception of His great love and plan for your life? How will you choose to live the rest of your life?

____

____

____

[45] The Living Bible copyright © 1971 by Tyndale House Foundation. Used by permission of Tyndale House Publishers Inc., Carol Stream, Illinois 60188. All rights reserved.

Thank the Lord that He has not only rescued you from the things of your past, but He is healing your broken heart and giving you a new heart full of His love for you. Ask Him to guide you today and every day to receive His love and then pass it on to those He brings across your path that have been bound by past shadows, poor decisions, painful experiences, shame, and confusion.

About the Author

Evangelist Rennee J. Johnson (Hubb) is a member of Victorious Life of Faith Church where Elder Victor L. Furr is the presiding Pastor. She is the leader of VLOFC Outreach Ministry (HAVE – Hope And Victory for Everyone) and serves with the Culinary Ministry. She assists with teaching Adult's Sunday school and the Dance Ministry.

Rennee J. Johnson (Hubb) was born on November 28, 1978, and was raised in the Prince George's County, Maryland. She has a deep passion and love for the youth and served over the Youth Ministry for several years.

She has recently started a catering business with her sister called Robin & Rennee' Catering.

She has two children, Kaviona and Keyon.